LAST

CORRESPONDENCE

∾

LAST CORRESPONDENCE

poems

∽

LELAND KINSEY

GREEN WRITERS PRESS   *Brattleboro, Vermont*

Printed in the United States

10 9 8 7 6 5 4 3 2 1

Green Writers Press is a Vermont-based publisher whose mission is to spread a message of hope and renewal through the words and images we publish. Throughout we will adhere to our commitment to preserving and protecting the natural resources of the earth. To that end, a percentage of our proceeds will be donated to environmental activist groups. Green Writers Press gratefully acknowledges support from individual donors, friends, and readers to help support the environment and our publishing initiative.

GReen
wrIters
press

Giving Voice to Writers Who Will Make the World a Better Place
Green Writers Press | Brattleboro, Vermont
www.greenwriterspress.com

ISBN: 978-09982604-9-5

COVER PHOTO GEORGEI KINSEY

PRINTED ON PAPER WITH PULP THAT COMES FROM FSC-CERTIFIED FORESTS, MANAGED FORESTS THAT GUARANTEE RESPONSIBLE ENVIRONMENTAL, SOCIAL, AND ECONOMIC PRACTICES BY LIGHTNING SOURCE. ALL WOOD PRODUCT COMPONENTS USED IN BLACK & WHITE OR STANDARD COLOR PAPERBACK BOOKS, UTILIZING EITHER CREAM OR WHITE BOOKBLOCK PAPER, THAT ARE MANUFACTURED IN THE LAVERGNE, TENNESSEE PRODUCTION CENTER ARE SUSTAINABLE FORESTRY INITIATIVE® (SFI®) CERTIFIED SOURCING

INTRODUCTION

෴

by Howard Frank Mosher

Leland Kinsey, often referred to as the poet laureate of Vermont's Northeast Kingdom, died of cancer on September 14, 2016. He was sixty-six years old. Having recently published a volume of his much-celebrated collected poems (*Galvanized*, Green Writers Press, 2016), Leland left behind two manuscripts: *Last Correspondence*, and an untitled sequence of poems, many written or revised during his last illness. This volume is a posthumous compilation of those two collections.

Last Correspondence, which was written over a period of four decades, is a rich poetic narrative, in letter format, between friends, lovers, and family members. Ranging from the vast deserts and ranches of the American Southwest, to the mountains and hillside farms of northern Vermont, and on to Labrador's taiga, with side excursions to Machu Picchu and the Isle of Skye, *Last Correspondence* evokes on every page Emerson's definition of "the kingly bard" who "must smite the chords rudely and hard."

Then come the incomparable "Final Poems," a cascade of stories, characters, and images, mostly from the Northeast Kingdom, and focusing on the recurrent themes of family, work, and place, which have run through Kinsey's poems from the start. Walt Whitman would have loved these poems, so, too, Robert Frost. They represent the finest works of a writer who will always be known as the truest voice of the remote and beautiful "kingdom" of Vermont settled by his Scottish ancestors seven generations ago, and preserved, in perpetuity, in hundreds of the most human and original poems in the history of American letters.

CONTENTS

~

LAST
CORRESPONDENCE

DANCE HYMNS

I lay beside you
in a city in the desert
and matched your breathing,
listening carefully,
knowing the child's secret
of not believing it can continue
until you are old enough to stop.

We had traveled to an arid climate,
but not together,
you to dance, I to write.
"Let your green eyes remind you of wetter lands,"
your letter said, and left it at that.
I wrote and spoke mostly of my wish
to see you; drove fourteen hours
for your greeting, nonplussed, smile.

I had driven all night under a gibbous moon.
The mist that crossed the road seemed
like ice haze from melting lakes or glaciers,
as from some past—recent or prehistoric—
that still holds in my thoughts of you.
Memories of you drift through
nights, ground into the convolutions.
I drove steadily but fast,
pushed toward an image
which never existed.

Deer and small animals seemed to line
the road. Luckily never a deer,
but often in the margins
a sudden reflection,
low eyes moving. I did not swerve,

I could not see the shoulder.
The sound of death punctuated
the language of that kind of travel.

The city threw a cover of light
over us, new to me though not to you,
and seemed to cast a glow
on nearby mountains. The lights are not supposed to reach
    there,
observatories scan opulent skies.
From the bed I read billboards
half-a-mile away.

In the studio where you danced
rather strict improvisational forms
under your teacher's guidance,
the lumber is yellow.
Your black tights highlighted the slightest
turn and counterturn.
Your motion and your body made me dizzy.
The room did not expand, became immense.
At the end of the day
we walked out onto the pebbles in the yard,
the landscape did not cease.

I did not see anyone
who reminded me of you.
We drove the regular grid
of houses, firms and schools,
the streets marked for high water,
out to winding passes,
flood marked at the entrances,
rising into the mountains.

Frost and heat have exploded rocks
white as the houses gathered
in the dusty city, or my home village.
The sun's disc declined,
we waited till dark to start back
toward a sky beyond which the gegenschein dissipated.

We returned to the city.
When I left the next day
a rainstorm swept in from the east,
cars and vendors' carts were washed away,
the floor of desert valleys flooded for miles
with water thick as spit.
Washes and arroyos held cars
bright as sores.

LETTER OF DESCENT

I

It is past autumn and not winter now.
I am writing this despite a promise
to myself to forget this season.
The trees outside are frenzied
with color and wind;
desire recreates their frantic appearance
in me. Your fingers are long and cool,
when they touch me I am numb where they descend.
The pattern of their descent has altered
like that of all winged things.
You told me of the geese you saw
while shelling in your garden.
I have never seen you there
Yet I picture you clearly,
legumes falling into an upturned palm.

II

I planted my crops late this year.
They came up straggly
in droughty raised beds.
I did not worry for I trusted fall,
not like a person, but as a careless season
that usually does not obliterate everything,
but gives one a chance to postpone loss.
It is only September and has frozen hard twice.
Already the flies are dying in my room.
They lay scattered over pots
of wilted flowers that I have decided not to water,
they also deserve this season,
their summer on my windowsills has been long.
Hummingbirds fed on their blossoms.
Weeks ago I watched the decrescendo of sparrows
as they flocked on the staff-like electric wires
before they fled from my garden
where they had bred and fed.
All winged things desert me now.
I have left my screens in;
my blankets are wet from morning fogs
and chill. You said I was cold.
I am a foolish martyr
to what I felt was prophecy

III

The geese do not descend for days.
They fly from the arctic across forests
larger than mass dreams,
across lakes like oceans gone wild,
across prairies where wheat fields
stretch so far a young man would wear out
his eyes searching for the end,
and above asphalt deserts where skyscrapers
stand dry and hard, wind twisted,
and people move like grains of sand.
The geese must rest, they lower toward my river,
my black pond. If they touch down
I will not remember them as they sink
into water like tar. I feel old;
the water is as stiff as I am.
I take a sickle and cut all the corn
that I planted by the pond.
My hands are red, wind bitten;
I flail them at the geese that still descend.

IV

The sky has many rooms
and all of them are empty.
The leaves have fallen, I burned
as many as I could.
Animals have descended to their burrows.
Insect swarms hide in stalks
and broken loam. Mud daubers gather
no more. Birds do not soar,
hawks and bluebirds have made their last
northern descents and now race south
against the sun, which is not in slow decline
but swift descent. The silence of falling things
comes to my ears. I do not cry out against anything,
but speak your name in a voice
that ranges from treble to bass.

REPLY TO DESCENT

I

I have thought of you often.
The mountains where I live seem like women
whose curves imitate my own,
curves which you have covered with your hands,
your hard hands that weld me to them.
You have been near me in dreams
that brought decay to the glass in my windows;
that made plants in my garden snap
from the cold, in mid-summer;
that took me through my bedroom door
into a city, and I went through a door
in the street to another city, and another,
and I knew you were in each;
you would have come to me then, but I would not let you
because you could not comfort me,
and you love.

II

The geese I saw above the mountains,
far above my garden,
were beyond sound, almost beyond vision.
I held my hand against the sun
as if staying it for a moment so I might see
those grey monuments brought low
by the intense heat, see them skim
the singed trees, then have them rise
beyond my vision. I told you of them
to keep from forgetting.
When I talk to you I will think of the geese,
quiet as you are.
When the geese were gone, the noise
I expected absent, my hands were free
once again to be filled with red beans,
warm and red like the viscera of geese,
bright red, so bright I had to look away.

III

I am in another city now,
a city familiar despite long absence.
There is a face, familiar, similar to my own,
my mother facing me across a room.
She is flushed.
We have returned from the ocean
where we ran. I remembered her.
The salt in the air said summer,
The water and grey sand on my feet said winter;
Nothing was said, I did not speak of you
and thought of you once while walking the dunes.
The city at our backs was like the shale cliffs
rising from where you and I swam.
My mother is singing what she sang
in lounges and bars,
songs I have sung to you, laughing.
She does not laugh; I will not sing to you.
A wind has risen; I close the window
as you should close yours to keep yourself warm.
You must listen to me, and not hear,
as I listen to my mother's voice
and forget what she sings.

IV

Back here I am cold;
I dance to keep warm.
Those I teach pay no attention;
they will not move to their own words
or understand a phrase as movement.
I left my blood in your house,
my body not quite even knowing itself
and you expect to know me so soon.
I went out with fishermen once, heard whales.
I yell at hills for the echo.
As a girl I played on an island
that has washed away.
Sound and movement are what I know;
you are still.

REWRITING

I

I wrote to you once late in the year,
but not as late as this.
It is heat's nadir. My fingers are stiff,
they inhabit my palms, but are not warm,
nor am I. Cars clot the highway.
They will not run and lay beached
on the shoulders like dying whales.
Trees are splitting, the cold snaps them
like perturbed bones. The long cracks
will seal and grow over, but never mend.
It is late night. Tomorrow I will work
with the men clearing fells,
re-opening roads and power lines.
I will send this in the morning,
a grey edge of words.

II

The snow is too deep this year.
The wild animals paw my land
for stubble and roots and never reach ground;
wander through woods,
browse small trees back to the trunks;
invade the suburbs, rattling cans,
graze on dry lawns, leaving tracks
no hunter sees. I ignore them
and their leaving. They scud through storms,
through nights, constantly pass my window.
I have no food for them.
The landscape is not barren,
it does not even seem so without you,
but it is far away, difficult to reach.

III

Birds leave tracks like runes
in the snow, or in the sand
by the ocean where you walked.
The language is indecipherable
but the image stays.
You spent a whole day among whales
that had driven themselves ashore,
monsters in the morning news,
dull witted as their patience slacked.
You did not watch them being cut up
and hauled away.
I see you, among rotting boulders,
trees encased in spray, sharply defined
like a word.

IV

The horizon is getting light.
The O-gape of snow craters
dominates the landscape; I read
nothing into it. I will not write
more of the animals, they are gone.
Or of the land locked in ice.
O you whose mouth was once molten.
The men are outside,
I will end this here.

LETTER OF WARNING FROM TWO CLIMATES

Reading that the theatre of the absurd
has lost its power, I try to think
of small dramas that I use
sardonically in writing that seems to fall
off at the end, like bricks placed carelessly
at the end of day,
or satellites that fall out of a winter sky,
that crater easily discerned
like a remnant trench from WWI
but in wide, though not empty, tundra

Your new house is out in the open

I am kept awake by the sound of dogs,
or perhaps a barred owl not so far off
I cannot follow the sound
with my eyes this late in the night,
depth perception of sound is lost in the wind

The cornices of snow are too sharp to remember,
but one at a time
I see you standing beside them,
dimly lit as on a late afternoon,
the sun shining through clouds
that have dropped no snow and will not
The hills are not blue,
it is the shade of your face in the distance,
I do not remember the center.
This is a poem about memory
and the memory is sufficiently dim
that I can write
with as few regrets as I can muster.
The street lights cast no shadows
though they are on.

The fact that nothing remains new
does not surprise us
but the fact of newness often does,
like a star in the tenth century
that outshined the moon,
and we talk about that and your house
The articles on our agenda prolong it
I stayed up two nights running
to see a comet reaching across a third of the sky,
and you slept, and both things
seemed equally astonishing,
the light and your sleep to come back to
I woke you and we quarreled

The entire sky seems alive with pigeons,
such a flock as went extinct a hundred years ago
They carry no messages
A century and more ago some might have had cameras
strapped to their breasts,
aerial views, of city streets, hedgerows,
washerwomen by rivers, framed by the tips of wings
    in the lens,
birds eye, fish eye, even the flutter of wings
stilled, the insistent urbanity
nestled even in war   My great uncle has a picture
of Paris from 1840 he got in the First World War
He claims the woman at the upper left
is a streetwalker, the only one who stood
long enough, the blurs are those who passed her by,
who had no money, or were going to work, or away.
The window is where he looked out on this
though much later By then people had started to take
pictures from zeppelins, then planes The pigeons outside
the windows of this city flap insistantly
The streets are incalculable when you do not come

Lakes have been riled most of the winter,
fish breathe with no ice
The stagnant layers from summer
re-oxygenated as water roiled in the narrows
the arched bridges span
Early in the year ice piled heavily
against the one on your outlet
You watched fatigue set in
and a section crumble
Fish in grey water could now breathe steel
and it reminded you of nothing
Some highways still lead nowhere
Fairs are packing and moving north,
the language of barkers shifting place,
syntax of maps and dying fish spawning

Satellites circle us
with an inanimate momentum we envy,
constantly falling toward us and away.
We watched the failed tracking experiment
where boron spewed across the night sky
like some dot to dot game writ large
All those paths were more intricate
than the map of city streets we searched
for an hour to find the restaurant
down past the museum that had closed
I wanted to show you the fabrics
made by Incas, and like yours,
or I said they were, but more the background
like the steps winding down by the side exit
into the street leveled by cranes
We ate outside in light rain,
Greek food in Arizona, the streets were noisy,
northern parts of the city had flooded,
people wondered if friends or family might drown

Underpasses of the city
are marked in feet for floodwaters
Bums have marked the height
where people drowned, some of them
went lightly, no change in pockets,
no cars with windows and doors
that wouldn't open underwater
We saw bodies on the sidewalk,
watched the sunset through rain clouds,
 the air over the dead bright orange
saguaro dreams of the city,
predator and prey We drove
to the national monument next day
I chopped a piece of cactus
for your souvenir We threw rocks
into a canyon, down at flying birds

Of no import this late in the season
there is little we have not brought forward
We refused the fire and the pension of the lost
We plow the ashes of our ancestors under
or they settle molecule by molecule into sediment beds
Few cliffs face north here, ancient ice created views
away from the coming cold, toward the oceans it reached
In the forests now acid rain and soil
eat the face of the remaining stone
These mountains separate me from you and do not vary
The sun sets in the west and I do not marvel at it
Colors bleed into land I cannot see
and that holds the light longer than here
Your house is higher than mine
and can maintain its hold
Mine slips eastward toward the sea toward the slope
that prefigures us

PLACEMENT

Stone by stone by stone
he loosens time and piles it up.
I'm paid to live with him to help him through,
a hard position for each of us.
He's up before me to cover his land
with pick and bar, choosing only
the right stones, and has them placed
before he's gotten them free.
He will not let me help; I listen.
"Cabot sailed in one small ship,
running his westing to a new land.
The Norse had come before
and many came after.
They sailed by latitude
and rough estimate.
Longitude's the hardest thing to find
to place oneself so that one knows."
He builds his stone walls north and south
to make his longitude exact he says,
to help others find out where they are.
He sounds the sky all day;
waits for the last light to come back
where the house harbors him.
His now miles of walls form
some kind of odd breakwater.
"I saw the aurora borealis once, showers
going up, light leaving the world."
He talks of discovery,
aches sometimes with a feeling
his walls will not help,
a second from his mind's old world,
a hundred and eighty degrees from his life.

THEORY OF TILES

I

Deer, turkey, antelope, quail
suffuse that dry terrain.
The only surface water for miles
flows on her land. Rock filtered, it rises
from huge springs,
then disappears after a four mile run
to rise much farther down
its outwash cut, the valley route aliens take
heading for surrounding ranches,
and towns, cities north of us.
They stopped at the house I had come to fix,
it rambles like a country fair.
They came for work in light clothes,
young men past eighty with children
that die before they do or grow without them.
They stand, each stands, hat in hand,
"¿Trabajar?" I do not understand
but shake my head. "¿Lunche?" I understand,
peanut butter, tortillas, agua con iello.
They sit in the yard, the odd clink of the ice in tumblers,
stratified and patterned bluffs
a distant backdrop on which they leave no sign
of passing. Indian drawings fade, are not lost.
An old woman across the gorge drew
pictures of a mummified child she found in caves.
The woman I worked with had such a drawing;
some of the men saw it, shook their heads,
moved north, any record or sense of record
in the act only, the natural history
of desire.

II

Vultures gathered in one tree
at the head of the river each dusk,
a small slow cyclone of return each evening.
We often startled them with our coming,
even though we paddled the canoe quietly
to where the river rose from springs
in the fractured limestone,
and their leaving was startling altogether,
as once was the fact that the man
she lived with was leaving.
I held her grey, and wet, and reeling
under wheeling shadows
made long as thunderheads.

III

In the land I left, the minister,
whose manse sits on land donated
by some ancestor or other, prayed
for me at my family's behest;
walked dark-shod
between pews where my grandmother,
grandfather, parents and relations
unto the nth remove sat rigidly.
Seen from above they would look like notes on a staff.
I heard them, continually I heard them,
and praised them and gave no attention.

IV

We found caves—sunken caverns—
below the floor of riffled valleys,
and skeletons in the caves:
Sheep heads, horns locked or alone,
eye sockets echoed the image of the surface hole;
the long backbones of snakes curled
or drawn straight, headless or fanged.
I imagine the wetbacks stopping here
in an occasional rain, backing under the overhang
just enough to avoid the storm's drive
and alive snakes, holding damp bundles
and themselves off moldy soil.
No animal can graze on stone.
What we do not know gnaws us,
bone chips in a bleached year.

V

A chimney blocks half the window
from where we would often lay.
The grout is crumbling, the window poorly framed.
Down to the left is a tree
which casts a shadow in the moonlight,
but the moon light had little to do with it,
the placement things mattered,
not image or meaning but mass.
My being there seemed as simple and complex
as a decision at a street corner,
which way back to work, which way home.

VI

At a tile makers, west of the Rio Grande,
Falling water, snails, small animals,
leaves and flowers in whole or part,
representational and geometric, a pattern
that is no pattern, shifted across two walls,
—how to choose when seeing that—
so she did not choose, she wanted the same,
she lacked a theory for periodic tiling.
The woman shop owner wrote on the back of each,
inscribing the clay with magic marker.
My friend translated, the shop owner did not smile
but would fake the slip for customs.
It did not matter, later we paid anyway,
we answered questions wrong. The car swayed
all the way back on sagging springs.
She was pleased, the tiles were authentic.

VII

A pair of shoes on the riverbank
and a man walking away barefoot
over sharp hot stones
miles from the border crossing.
The shoes are no good
and the man is worn,
but there is no comparison, cast off, poor,
every image drops down foolishly.
The dust rises, covers mesquite and juniper.

VIII

She was working on a print
etching a bat's wing, birds
flying low over water. I stood
hand on the door in shadow.
She spoke. "Don't worry, I like to feel this way."
I did not move or answer. It was not light out.
Her father had been dead two years;
she had not cried since then
and little then. "You can't help."
She moved rapidly, burin towards me.
My hand came out of the darkness
and struck her. She stood, I turned,
sun came through the window,
the non-periodic pattern a triptych,
the order was our own and broken.

LONG CORRESPONDENCE

The aliens still come along the river
but because we are at the ranch so seldom
they do not stop as often,
the invisible network that is theirs
makes us invisible.
We hear them at night
talking beneath the oaks.
The oaks, weakened by air moss,
are dying of live oak disease.
The pecans are withering in opened stands.
The first settler's cabin has finally fallen in.
It is too hot to even swim.
I saw you five times last year.

＞

When I left I brought pecans
and those seed pods from the cave
I found them in my desk yesterday
the rattle was difficult to bear
like the layer of leeches on my legs
from the lake outlet where we swam
One by one you picked them off
and your fingers were like my own
after raspberrying as a child
We were pleased by the cave's
long-legged spiders undulating en masse
along the crevices and ceiling
It bothered your mother that the history
of my family here was longer
than that of settling there
my sense of place less necessary

The horses on the ranch have learned to open
the bump gates, we are always finding them by the river
When they see us coming they jostle
back through the gate
into the field where we hunted butterflies
for your young friend,
The neighboring rancher was irrigating the fields
you would not have recognized them
but with this long drought
the water's too low and the salts came out
and killed everything, even the cactus
In the bottoms of the gorges we often see dirt twisters
whose tops just reach the level of the plateau

        ∼

I read in the news they are arresting
more and more Mexicans, but many times
more than they can catch are coming
Your ability to understand them always amazed
them and me and you would ask them for words
to explain their plight to them
We mixed salt and sugar and soda one night
to give a man too long in the sun
Those we hired to dig the long ditch
asked us to mail letters home   long mud-smudged envelopes
The fact of writing such as those
made my writing seem unreal, as though they wrote of Cortez
or the first explorers
Medicos   postales
I never feel as useful now   When making love
we sometimes didn't answer them
their slowly repeated knocks

the push of grass like an armadillo's earthmoving
I hope you've let the garden go
Mounding the soil we brought from the river
I, we both, knew it wouldn't work

I am painting again and very tired
but not the six-month's tiredness before I married
How I repeat myself   this necessity for work
the willingness you helped me build
for disregarding everything but this
I did not get your letter
till we returned from camping on the Rio Grande
I cried
It is in the closet under a stack of copper
for my prints

Send the poems I wrote on to Julie
She asked to see some the day
we three swam to Last Bath Creek
I remember the weakness in our legs
and her uncomfortableness that you and I were so soon lovers

When he left and you stayed the pattern
moving had assumed altered
there was no crush on me to gather everything
and he left almost everything behind
so I still packed it   later   For the first time
in five moves I found no playing card
One had always been somewhere on a floor
though neither of us played

Julie is not bothered now or really then
but she almost loved you too
and that was hard for both of us
You made what I did and said seem important   addressed me
with attention

~.

Went lepidoptering with my friend
we were stopped by an afternoon storm
but not one like that with nine kinds of lightning
in an hour you and I watched rise behind the hills
or your first meteor shower   you turned and said
It's like the last day of my life
We found that antler of lightning fused sand by the river
You're a face in a moving car now
windshield-obscured
speaking mostly a language I understood little
did not learn more
medicos   postales
On the last day of our last meeting
you put the side of your palm
between your breasts and said
It feels like just this part of a hand is pushing here
It was
I wish my letters could eat away copper and zinc
I wish I'd mailed more letters from those ditch-stained hands

INK-FIXED

In the mail today your etching
and the dead butterfly
Spring comes early there
here late snow clings
almost rain
The daub of printer's ink
the butterfly mistook
    caught close-winged
    by one quick spreading mimicry
had dried red and hard
by the time it arrived
Grey dapples and the orange
of the only wing showing.

This last fall when you began
painting I wondered how you would handle
the question of mimesis
This last abstract self-portrait
from a run of fifty
moving toward singular acts
attracts me
The apparatus of and for the seasons
don't change
My eye that must focus
or miss everything
is a screen limiting staying
constant seizure
as is the delicate balanced drum
inside my head

as are you words and images
become you
The evolution of my life is slow
tedious and wondrous with detail
outside these sudden clear mutations

SWITCHEL

is the name of the recipe
I mixed that day for the Salvadorans
you had found on your morning run
hiding under the mescalbean scrub.
The family of five had walked, bused,
trucked, walked again to our small audience
by a dry riverbed in West Texas.
Since we didn't have many supplies
laid up I thought it would be okay.
When I was a kid,
field work, hand work in the fields,
occasioned it; muggy hot days
when we had to turn
rain-dampened windrows
bottom to top with pitchforks
to dry them right—the one long roll
of hay in a large hay field
made for miles of work at a step-turn pace,
like prisoners working a roadside;
or when a thousand bales lay
ready for picking up, to be handled twice,
once off the stubble and once in the loft;
or a newly bulldozed or plowed piece
lay cobbled with stones to be cleared.
Mother or grandmother would produce
a jug of switchel, water, vinegar, molasses,
ginger, mixed for a drink that made your throat sting
like your outside sun-struck skin,
and the vinegar sometimes caught
in your windpipe for a coughing fit.
Even then I thought better to have the rum
my New England ancestors traded for,

pour in some hard cider for stonewall,
than to stand, forsaken and angry,
ready to strike out, drinking switchel.
Better to stand away, let me suck it
from a sponge at the end of a stick
for some kind of salvation.
What mixed emotions you and I had
as we watched that revivified family walk
over the hill with what little they had on their backs.

ARMY WORMS

I noticed the soft crunching first,
billions of jaws devouring the rowen,
necessary fodder in this drought season.
The sound is like horses eating hay
from a manger, or listening to a field
of corn grow on warm humid nights,
the rustle of expansion;
or like the rub of taffeta against my leg
at prom balls in my earlier life.

Crows gathered in fall-like flocks,
fed till they were so fat they could not lift off,
black sacks of caterpillars bundling about
on legs that could barely hold them.
After the egg-laying, the crows
scratched after the eggs so hard
that kale started to sprout in late summer,
a feathery green on bald soil.

Some fields, like the sorghum,
where we sprayed the periphery, we saved.
We mowed one as the infestation moved across it,
and raked and baled the farther third.
But most we lost, a thin winter coming.
It reminds me of the white marble ballroom
animated forty years earlier
by swing bands playing for patrons
of expensive whores
in the hotel just over the Rio Grande that we closed
one night. A coolness rose up from the floor
sunk below the stage like a small quarry,
the chill coming in from the edges;
nothing for us to do
but leave.

FISH EGGS

So you fished each of the Three Forks,
rediscovering The Corps' discovery.
I wish I could cover those waters with you.
Yes, I went to Labrador again,
fished the upper reaches of the Atikonak
for brook trout, *grande rouges* they call them,
and ouananiche. My arms ached
one day from catching and releasing.
I landed one towards day's end
in a long fast riffle, as others swam
upstream, backs out of the water,
between my legs and all around.
I slipped the two long sets of eggs
out of the belly of the big red,
and set them on a rock.
The eggs had the color and look
of the drupelets of cloudberries
I'd gathered in my creel
at the edges of string bogs.
The eggs and berries were to be my gift
to the Inuit woman
who cooked my evening meals.
I turned to wash the spine blood
from my catch, half a minute,
and when I turned back, a gull sat
where the eggs had been,
a slight gel coating beneath its webbed toes.
Eggs, and no gull noticed,
gull, and no eggs to be seen,
no one's rights involved,
just, quick as that,
life's magic
act.

COFFEE

At church suppers the women
would carry the coffee maker,
that seemed as big as a steam packet boiler,
from the kitchen to the shelf
in back of the hall where the line
would form for what smelled
like rich earth baking, but for us,
the children, was forbidden.
The farmers and wives of my large family
sat in chairs at oak tables stained dark
and spoke of a world dark as coffee, but close.

Tonight I brewed one cup in my own house
and thought of the half hot water
half hot milk coffees you used to make us.

A woman relative returned from Bogotá
years ago and spoke to the parishioners
about her twelve years in the mountains
where men carried burlap bags
the size of their lungs, and steep
prices did not filter down.
Your letter of traveling to Machu Piccu,
your altitude sickness, made me think of this.
Her fingers were stained from the beans,
but she said not much was drunk there,
the workers chewed coca leaves, a palliative
she said, and that they needed aid.
I would have wished them well
against her arguments,
as someone who can fly or sail away.
And, if she return, bring money,

clothe, heal, be persuasive.
She was later shot in Pakistan.

My Armenian friend, with whom I first drank
coffee, made it strong and black
with lots of sugar boiled right in,
then dumped the thick frothing mixture
from the *cezve* into tiny cups.
For Masters exams we studied Johnson and Boswell
who almost dwelled at coffee houses,
whose lives came to something,
who knew man was a little thing.

In recent years coffee crop failures
drove producers to demand higher prices,
caused countries to organize. I rationed
myself, but was only poor here.
I remember my once-removed cousin's
wooden hands on my face.
My parents could not afford me shoes that summer.
"You're so lucky to be well off," she said,
and I knew it was so. My Highland and lowland ancestors
had been able to flee
and become what we so seldom are,
not necessarily giving, or generous, or kind,
but community.

You, your body as warm and curved
as this cup in my hands, lie far away.
I am also thinking of faces of adults around long tables
talking of their lives,
if not with hope, at least its close cousin.

burned. The toys that survived
ravages of youths are ashes now,
sacred ashes maybe, but ashes,
some carried aloft in the stiff winds off the Minch,
the rest sodden from the rains those winds bring.
The woman owner lives now without
home or income. My kids begged
to stop there each of the years
 we've been to Skye.
The woman had played with many
of the toys as a child, collected more
and played with all. Her father played
with many of them as a child,
her grandfather some, whose stiff father
brought and bought his boy
little joy, his few toys like new.
Jacob's ladders raced in her fingers,
or formed the entire alphabet.
An erector set on a large scale
built into tower and cantilever
must have set young men's minds
to building the drop dead bridges
Scots flung across the world's rivers.
The remains of model and pedal cars,
flung just as madly
about the floors by young men
who would later swing the real ones
under the checkered flags of all nations,
lie as sintered heaps now.
And the dolls, bisque-headed, oaten-haired
lie cremated, as do the horses with spikes
back facing on their hooves

so they only sped forward
on the clattering canvas track.
All bets are off. With the game done
memory tightens like a Chinese finger puzzle
one might not wish to get clear of.
The road to the lighthouse
built by two hundred men in two years,
a hundred sawing stone
from the sea cliffs full time,
passes hard by the ashen hole,
and for anyone who knew the house,

lies longer, more drear,
and the children have the sense,
as I often do in my writing,
of losing something even before it is dear.

A POEM TO ONE

You are right, I tell you more,
and I suppose it is
because you love me and I love her
and I want to write to both of you.
I well know it's harder,
as you say,
for some than others.
I enclose a poem you will recognize
parts of yourself in.

THE WOMAN WHO RODE

In these northern Appalachians
she rode back roads, farmers' fields,
high pastures, through hunter-jumper enclaves,
and rhododendron thickets. In Texas she would ride
as far and never leave her father's ranch,
broken grasslands, yellow hills, gullied roads.
Growing up with her mother
in the east, she handled high steppers,
show jumpers, hunters on trial
across manicured grounds.
Sometimes during stays in Mexico
it got harder, learning to ride
and jump without reins, to tumble
and leave no permanent bruises,
no broken bones.
For months each summer
she rode her father's land hard,
saddle or no, bridle or no,
just hands in the mane.
She rode with the *vaqueros*
rounding up cattle and angora goats,
checking the lines, crossing *los rios*,
swimming them too, with the horse or alone.
Thirty years later, husband watching,
she can still drive
a herd across hard terrain
and put them through difficult gates alone,
wishing her father there to see it.
Her husband tried to learn to ride,
fell several times, though not as hard
as he fell for her. Her father wished
his sons by other mothers,

who had her ability,
matched her ease and will.
He taught her to shoot, she could hit
a nickel on the fly.
His sons will sell the land in trust for them.
She would have kept it,
the names on the deeds the same.
On a relative's land she once rode
the northern Sonora, rode out of Chihuahua.
She's one who could have ridden
with Pancho Villa, or with Tom Horn,
won hearts of the west, or stolen them,
broken them like sticks,
tinder for a campfire on the Chisolm Trail.
She would have been as dangerous
or as selfless as she wanted to be,
as the shot out eyes of Jefferson and Indians
attest, many a buffalo shot clean through.
Such a one would have had offers
from husband or raider or cowboy or thief:
Let's round them in early;
Let's number our losses;
Let's count our booty;
Let's bed down here, let's bed down here.
What will be offered is what memory brings:
a boulder strewn river washing off
the dust of cattle under the skull-shaped outcrop
of rock overlooking Last Bath Creek;
the smell of a creosote-stained house
in the shade of a huge pecan
after a day too long on the range.

LAST POEMS

MOLASSES

Putting molasses in the beans,
my great-grandmother's recipe,
spilled some on my shirt
and licked it off
and I was in the barn vestibule
with the drum of low-grade
acrid molasses we put
on hay, from a wet season
that had dried dusty
with mold and even
hungry cows turned up their snotty
noses. I carried
our old flower sprinkler
with nail enlarged holes
over each manger.
The concrete under the bay
built up a sticky patina.
We kids would stick our finger
up the bung hole formed mouth
then into ours;
the sulfur taste lasting
longer than the sweet
like popcorn balls and cookies.

A MOMENT'S NOTICE

The Wheeler Mountain fire tower's gone
the leather leaf is leather leaved.
A Lincoln sparrow whispers its song.
The quaking bog is sinking under me
where I kneel picking cranberries;
chewed piles mark southern lemming runs.
I could sink through this floating
sphagnum mat to bedrock scoured
down by glaciers only a few millennia
since.
A moose feeds in the deeper channel
completely under except when he snorkels
up his lugubrious head.
Every red and jade pitcher plant
that hasn't collapsed like an old sac,
is brimmed by
recent rain.
Small arched cranberry vine rises from
crimson moss-covered hummocks,
the bases of cedars killed in
lumbering times by the squirt dams
that flooded this basin.
Old Man's beard leans in a blustery
wind that's taking the red Labrador
tea leaves. White-striped bog rosemary
stands short, stiff and green.
Muskrats are shredding cattail rush
To heighten lodges and store for food.
Mountain fly honeysuckle's twigs are
bare and grey like the high hardwoods
over which ravens fly and croak.
I soon stand and re-commence
my vast lifetime journey towards you.

AFTER THE FOGS

That I rode my motorcycle through
arriving cold and wet at school
to see you.
Wetness of November gives way
to dry air of January and February
so dry it can shrink
and warp the hardest grained woods
my fine old house contracts
crinkles the horse hair plaster
a little, new hairlines
would be apparent if I looked
for them.

BONXIES

At Eshaness, my daughter found
two eggs pale aqua
marked as if with dipped tar,
opened and eaten on the fly.
Guillemot eggs snatched by skuas
winged acrobat predators of cliffs
and skerries. Called Bonxies
in the Shetlands. They'll bonk
you good if you get too close
to nest or mate and one knocked
my pie cap off my head,
the worker's cap, what my grandmother
called my "go to hell hat"
for the way I looked out from under its brim,
flew a ways in the wind
and I traipsed fast after it
with newly watchful eyes
as the same and other skuas
came in low for attack.
I swung my raincoat to ward
them off, they got clear of the ground.
My daughter had been yelling
warning, she laughed when I reached
her, a girl's laugh
but with tears in her eyes.

BROTHER ANDRE'S HEART

Beyond the chapel a reliquary of St. Joseph,
in a brick sarcophagus on the first floor,
walls lined floor to ceiling with crutches, wooden legs and
    arms,
metal legs and arms, and now titanium and carbon
legs and arms, left as thanks,
up escalators
toward the dome overlooking the backside of
Mont Royal, facing away from the river
that gave the city its life, we came
to the manikin room of a brother's life
and shown is one facing the hill where
he longed to build the oratory and
one of him on his bed just before some
kind of ascension and opposite is a vial
of oil embedded in the wall his backlit
heart taken out for some other
good, raising further alms to raise the
dome to St. Joseph when Brother Andre's
heart beats the old world and just plain
old relics all to hell for draw.

CROWD TALKING

A rare May day
everyone out in the air
the yellow warbler expresses it best
"sweet, sweet, oh so sweet"
and the warmth makes everyone pleasant.
The chestnut-sided greets "pleased, pleased, pleased
   to meet cha"
and compliments abound
The robin seems aware of the spring-bright colors
and youngsters' angst
"pretty boy, pretty boy, cheer up diddle"
for who could be sad on such a day
kids playing; school about over
and the ovenbird tutored speaker
who has learned the call on his return
"Teacher, teacher, TEACHER"
She builds her oven nest
in the forest debris
The song sparrow opens Beethoven's Fifth
in the orchard again and again
like endless practice
and parula's nest in the lichen
Old Man's beard wishing for a tent
to "ziiiiip up" as clouds build
toward rain, spring's must
The olive-sided flycatcher in fancy vest is
ready on the wing but grounded
as evening comes "Quick three beers"
The snipes "who who who who" winnow of wings
like wind in high wires—

The woodcock's tremulous whistle
Goatsuckers calling for punishment
of the universal scapegoat "whip-poor-will whip-poor-will"
   in ceaseless vengeance
and the tufted titmouse "peter, peter, peter, here, here, here"
   calling him in
or pointing him out
to the rest of the crowd.

MAPS

Half the railways of England race toward the crazy window
of my bedroom, the northern counties, borders,
and all of Scotland cut from the map
to fit. Still my bedroom though I haven't slept
there for twenty years. Still my maps,
though mother papered the walls
with them while I was away at school.
The bookmobile delivered addresses
in books, magazines, flyers,
to our remote farming village
and I sent away to mining outfits,
the world's railroads, tourist boards,
shipping concerns for the maps
I felt I needed, as well as the ones
the librarian gave me from National Geographic.
I studied them hard
in my short free time on the farm,
not as a route to get out,
but to know exactly where I lived
and could live. The world's geography
slumped off my bureau, wedged open the drawers,
covered my chair, papered the floor.
I returned one vacation to find
the wide world pasted to my walls
and me the small center
of a diminished thing.
The slanting light from the slanting window
Reached only a third of the world each day,
the rest lay in a penumbral shadow,
tropical isles in polar dark, pure white Antarctica
swept each day by the white heat

of the morning sun. Sri Lanka lay east
of Brazil. The survey map of northern India,
whose triangulations seemed to culminate
in the world's highest peak, abutted
the border incognita of Labrador and Quebec.
I, angry for the collection lost,
upset at the information gone,
strained to some limit trying to make
whole what could be seen,
right at home.

MOTHER'S MOTHER

died five days ago
buried two ago
under a stone that had her name
for thirty years—
after my grandfather died,
her patience just as stony.
Today I took from the house
in the general sharing
a large yellow bowl
a forty year old rex begonia
ugly as some sins;
and a metal measuring scoop
blackened with burnt fat.
She used to test if the melted lard
was hot enough by dropping a match
on its surface. If the match lit
she'd clap on the cover to extinguish
the flaring then begin frying doughnuts—
for family and summer folks
who'd never tasted the like.
She'd dip out debris and lower globs of lard in
to melt as the level dropped.
I cooked the enclosed doughnuts
in the arch while boiling in
the day's sap. They're pretty good.
I'm difficult to be with, I know
because like you,
always at the kindle point.

MOUNTING TIRES

When I was a kid
we slid off roads
and walked home
or couldn't make hills
and walked home
or crashed into cars and trees.
Now I beggar our budget
for the best tires made.

NIGHT STROLL

Walked overstreet this October night,
cold night, rain, scuffing leaves,
river running deep under the small bridge.
You and I walked out into the city
late on a night like this,
ponchos pulled tight
we crossed the street from the apartment
where you lived and moved
down Bridge street, iron arch span
black as your eyes, wide
in the dim light. Street lights
through trees made concentric circles.
The river slapped granite abutments
and the sides of its rickrack channel
and ran on under buildings beyond.
We could still smell the leaves
in the sidewalk green belt,
the tang of fall like the woods
I hunted in as a kid.
We passed the dimly lit windows
of closed businesses,
your face illuminated orangeish
like the lower parts of certain trees
we passed under. I thought about
the damp basements and sub-basements
levels down beyond knowing well.
The trains left a smell of electricity.
The easy metaphor would be
the electricity between us
the deep running current,
but it was the wondrousness

of being alone in a crowded place,
those who had ventured out,
mostly tucked in clubs and eateries,
and those who had not, all aware
of the edge those scuds gave
the night and season.
Our arms tucked through the other's

ORA AND ONA

Brother and sister may live
side by side
but each as celibate and separate
as one day from the next
although they touch.
Each day as old
as the earth is old
and as fresh
as an infant's first caught breath.
The days unfold slowly
for us now.
Age does not rush.

OUT

My older brothers would come in early Friday nights, polish their white bucks and set them aside to dry. No touching them with dirty little fingers and toes. Then they'd go up to bathe and dress and come back down looking brand new and smelling good. When I'd ask when they were going they'd smile big brother smiles and say, "Out." Well, their out was a whole lot different than my out. When I stepped out the door nothing much changed, but they went to movies, which I didn't know what they were, but was told by them was like having pictures for the radio programs we all listened to in the evening when all chores were done, and dances with live music, which was played in our house and grandma and grandpa at the piano or organ with the boys on guitars and harmonicas, but no dancing as grandma's and grandpa's church, which they still attended after the schism, didn't allow and, though Mom and Dad went to the new church which allowed, if with sufficient decorum, we all honored the old tenet in our grandparents' presence.

PARTRIDGE

My dog frisks out
Across the pasture
to the apple orchard edge,
nose in leaves and holes,
eyes up. He's the brindle
of chestnut leaves of which a few
still exist in this wood.
He freezes as I come up slow

till almost under foot the ruffed grouse
rises here called partridge
and I take him on a quartering lead.
My dog doesn't jump at the gun.

REPAIRING THE SAPLINES

My uncle hired a logger
to clear his sugar orchard of aging maples,
those over-tapped, ice-damaged,
giving light and room
to vigorous replacements.
The logger lived in a tar paper shack
with a dozer outside the size of his house.
He would cut for days,
then make a day of hauling out
with that crawler that cost like hell to run
but could run over, push through
any obstacles.
He wore brown wool pants,
brown toque, brown monkey-face gloves
and always streaks of tobacco juice
down each sharp crease
from a frowning mouth.
Said he could tell if a log had bird's-eye,
sold it to furniture makers,
and cut off all burls
of which many swelled from the bolls of that aging forest
and sold them to turners.
My uncle's tariff wasn't stiff
but the logger never seemed to have money;
a series of ten dollar cars run for a month
and abandoned,
inspection required after thirty days;
who had a hermit's habits
but wanted company.

SHRIKE AND CARDINAL

The shrike dove through the spruce
tree and drove the cardinal
out of there and followed
at such a rate I thought
surely had the red blur
but the cardinal swerved
into a white cedar
and sat fast—hidden.
The shrike shuttled back
and forth through the warp
of the tree. The cardinal
held at this fell line
not willing to die
the small-faced woof as the shrike
sought to card him with his claws.

STEEPLE CLOCK

We've purchased a house
whose upper windows overlook
the village and three steeples
one with a clock night-lit
on a hill that's the local
high point for long haul freight trains,
midnight bells and crossing horns
especially clear on damp nights.
As a child I'd sometimes go
with children's Missionary group
to view an elderly man's clock.
Its purpose was a clock
but the actual clock was small
as a child's mouth,
open in magazines, as the clock chimed
from a steeple in the picture.
The church in the picture topped
the village. A woman swung her arm
in the foreground
casting invisible seed
to a half dozen chickens,
that peck, peck, pecked deliberately starved day round,
as they have been fed
for almost two hundred years
though the owner thought four hundred;
a carriage in the middle ground passed
regularly between two copses of trees
and down to the left a man pulled
a fish from etched glass rippling water
every quarter hour;
and because the man's house
had never been wired
night was still dark in that village

even lantern lit
but the clock chimed urgently,
the carriage traveled from darker shadow
to darker shadow
arrival ever anticipated,
the morning chores never done,
and the fish came ashore
in biblical numbers lush
enough to fertilize the valley
pastures pictured,
The family story poured
out each time, each time
a slightly different riverlet
the escape from enclosure;
a sea journey tinted every shade of green;
how hard to cart the large picture clock,
a missing bowed-glass corner
lost enroute.
This valley is busier;
farms wider;
the river larger
which I stalk for trout
like even the ancient Egyptians
who loved angling.
Trains and tractors pass at all hours;
and the clock abiding in this steeple
also its many gears
lit by river-dam power
for a hundred years
and the glass in my windows
slumping
to ripple the present view,
humdrum or vibrant
old as time.

THANKSGIVING KITE

I let a kite out before the meal.
My parents, grandparents, fourteen aunts and uncles,
brothers and sisters and twenty-six cousins trooped
out to see it beyond the pasture
swirls of snow wedged in the stone wall's shade
the wind died down awhile
and after the family meal I flew the kite again
beyond the yard and brook and the neighbor's field
about a mile of string
the eye couldn't follow, but I tugged
with no response, then tied
to the barb wire fence
as we all said our goodbyes.
Three weeks later my grandmother called
to say the kite was flying
with the light wind coming through
almost at the zenith when I arrived
the kite easily lifted the rock I tied on
to give it the lift to fly free.

THE SWAMP

Posted for years
where I hunted new calves,
where sister and brother and I
waded the small slow streams
kicking up silt in corner pools
in order to see the tiny
transparent fish swim
near the surface where
we could catch them
in our hands
and bottle them up for a time.
Open again for hunting
the deer yard
where they winter over
in the dense cover
of fir, spruce, hemlock and cedar
where they slip like a comb
through hair, but a hunter
can get all tangled,
the paths, with scrapes
and rubs marking the way
and efts on the mossed corduroy
logging roads lie scattered
like saffron.

WARMTH

This farmhouse where I live now
built on courses of coarse stone
lining a cellar kept from freezing
by the earth's moderation.
Everything always could freeze:
water on my winter bureau;
pipes up from the spring;
fresh milk set in the pantry to cool.
My father used spruce boughs to bank the
part of the wall that rose
and became foundation,
laying and intertwining the cut boughs
as prickly as hell.
I've sprayed foam over the rocks
inside and three feet below grade,
replaced sawdust in stud bays
with recycled paper blown in,
laid the attic with felt and fiberglass.
Not a whit of the work willingly done
but for the threat and thrall of cold
and a kind of love,
knowing still everything always could freeze.

WE'RE PILING ALONG

my friend, his son and I,
the north shore of the St. Lawrence
at three hundred miles an hour,
so I'm writing this jittery note
as something might get back
and if I do I'll remember.
We're up near where the first
Europeans entered the continent.
We've been fishing up near Ungava Bay
north of the tree line,
where barren grounds and black bears
are fierce as the landscape.
Brook trout move like red torpedoes
and caribou migrate, heeled by
arctic wolves that can carry
a haunch with head held high.
We're taking the taxi
at the airline's expense
because the plane dropped
out of fog, goosed it
and rose back into fog,
leaving us stranded in St. Havre.
We'll make the morning connection
in Sept-Iles.
            Pointing to a house
on a wild outcrop over the river
as wide as the sea,
the taxi driver says,
"the fat woman of the North
lives there," his only acknowledgement
in a hundred thirty miles of travel.
Lower down, we cross at Moise
great salmon river of the east

and in dusk's last wash of light,
a fisherman stands on a boulder
in a wide cascade, his long
rod doubled by the pull
of some great fish he's trying to keep
out of the fastest water and from loss.
The dark hills hazed with mist
have the form and color
of caribou as they shouldered
their way out of the tundra pond
onto the narrow peninsula
where we stood as they streamed by.
We watched them enter
the pond like three tributaries
into the larger water course
and keep formation all the way
across and gathered and ran
in columns one so close
we had to step back
from wide antlers,
large eyes noting us but
not shying.
When the float plane came
late to take us out,
I stood just aft of the propeller
to watch for strays, or unmapped
rocks as we taxied the whole
length to face the wind
for takeoff on this pond the pilot
cursed for size and as we
rooster-tailed at full throttle,
worried a straggler cow or calf
would rip a pontoon right off

but we cleared the water and barely,
the trees.
      The road's too wet
for the tires to squeal but
we're at the limit of adhesion.
I guess my choice would be
the lashing brackish water
at the foot of the cliffs we top
rather than them.

PHOTOGRAPHING CHRIST'S STATUE

Beside a dirt road,
dusty because frozen
in the late fall,
Christ stood
at the edge of a now pasture,
once field, on a once farm
now cellarhole and defunct barn.
Tall, sere, wind-tracked grass
ran to a field line of maple—
bird cherries, wild plum, apple trees
bare as the armature wires
exposed by head and limb loss.
The one extant was extended
as if in benediction.
The two remaining fingers tracing
the air as it drove past
Plaster the color of the icy clouds
that rose behind rare passing cars and trucks
lay in exfoliated pieces and chunks
chipped by shotgun blasts
that thoroughly patterned the robed torso
mostly where the heart would have been
I went and returned with my grandmother's
bellows camera she received as a gift
in the early part of the century.
My grandfather would tie a string
to the eyeletted shutter button,
thread it through the pivoted
piece built for it and
setting the camera on its built-in
tripod; run it to where
the family stood in descending

order to be pictured, and
tie it to his ankle
as its hidden trip when all
were ready. Often in the exposures
one of more of the children
are watching the line.
This day I close the iris only partway,
the low rolling clouds keeping
the light a mid-grey
and the softwoods behind the deciduous line
almost black mid-day; and set the stop.
   A friend was teaching pin-hole camera
   classes, oatmeal boxes and pierced tin foil
   doing the same as this elaborate
   bellows and box. I'll trust my hand
   counting exposure times.
I enclose a contact print
I haven't made enlargements
you can see some details are clear
others out of focus.
Well-defined cumulo nimbus budding
where the head should be;
the wind whispering through the grasses
and weeds, murmuring louder
in the forest, could have been its
missing voice—large and largely empty,
but forceful in its conversing
a fragment of this blessed day
worth sending to you.

DISMANTLING A TREE

Wedged between a house
a highway wire
and an ancient church
the weeping willow shaded all of them
before its dying.
Planted by the father
of the elderly homeowner.

A sawyer lops away the branches
releases them to fall to one side.
He finishes the cut to the trunk
for a vertical fall missing all.
Roofs, wiring, church, passing traffic.
Lightning topped it
twenty feet gave a false top
edging up the side.

Norwegians topped pines a thousand years
ago left them standing till only the heartwood was good
and built stave churches
that still stand.
Xylem, phloem. I think
how the sawyer must know
which way the wind is blowing
on this gusty day
that as aphorism
with so many and hard sways
will not catch him
on his safety rope.
Hits the larger pieces
lowered by rope around the bole
hits dead fall pulley.
His chain saw hangs from a short

sling like a gunfighter's weapon
and he deftly swings it into action
with one hand the other holding
limb from falling on limb to keep
his limb from dislodging him from his
spiked boots.

Now he's topping what the lightning
left, working his safety strap
saw length by saw length
keeping the saw from jumping back.
He sets his spikes securely
each time swaying in arms
his wedge of sky.

~

CPSIA information can be obtained
at www.ICGtesting.com
Printed in the USA
LVOW12s0922130517

534370LV00004B/6/P